Hacking

Basic Hacking Fundamental Secrets,
How to Hack

Steven Dunlop

DEDICATION

This book is dedicated to my beautiful and loving
girlfriend, Danni.

CONTENTS

ACKNOWLEDGMENTS

The insights in this book have been passed down to me from a number of inspirational people who I have had the good fortune of meeting. This book could not have been written without you and my life would not be on the path it is now. I am eternally grateful to everybody who has positively impacted my life and I wish to share your wisdom here in these pages through my words. Thank you to all, you know who you are..

DISCLAIMER

No part of this publication may be reproduced or transmitted in any form by any means, mechanical or electronic, including photocopying or recording, or by any information storage and retrieval system, or transmitted by email without permission in writing from the publisher. Reviewers may quote brief passages in reviews.

While all attempts have been made to verify the information provided in this publication, neither the author nor the publisher assumes any responsibility for errors, omissions, or contrary interpretations of the subject matter herein.

This book is for entertainment purposes only. The views expressed are those of the author alone, and should not be taken as expert instruction or commands. The reader is responsible for his or her own actions.

Adherence to all applicable laws and regulations, including international, federal, state, and local governing professional licensing, business practices, advertising, and all other aspects of doing business in the US, Canada, or any other jurisdiction is the sole responsibility of the purchaser or reader.

Neither the author nor the publisher assumes any responsibility or liability whatsoever on the behalf of the purchaser or reader of these materials.

Any perceived slight of any individual or organization is purely unintentional.

INTRODUCTION

This book will teach you the basic ideas and concepts related to computer hacking. It will discuss the fundamentals of hacking, the two types of hackers, the tools used by professionals, etc. By reading this material, you'll become familiar with the skills, programs, and techniques used by hackers in attacking computer networks.

The book you're reading aims to train you to become a white-hat (also known as ethical) hacker. Thus, you will use your knowledge and skills to help businesses and organizations enhance their digital security.

Thanks again for purchasing this book, I hope you enjoy it!

CHAPTER 1

HACKING – AN OVERVIEW

Hacking is the process of altering the software and/or hardware of a computer to accomplish things that are outside of the user's real purpose. The term "hacker" applies to individuals who engage in hacking activities. Thus, if you use any hacking tool or technique, you will be tagged as a hacker regardless of your objective.

Hacking is extremely popular among teens and young adults, although some old people dabble with these activities too. Most hackers are IT buffs who love to know more about computers and think of hacking as a form of art. These people know one or more programming languages and possess advanced skills in terms of network administration. For these people, hacking is a great way to apply their knowledge and technical skills. They consider hacking activities as opportunities to show their skills, not chances to perform malicious stuff.

Many hackers work independently. However, some businesses and organizations actually hire hackers as members of their IT personnel. These hackers, commonly known as white-hat or ethical hackers, utilize their tools and abilities to strengthen their employer's digital security. They help in detecting and fixing the vulnerabilities present in the network.

Two Types of Hackers

According to computer experts, hackers are divided into two types: white-hat and black-hat. Let's discuss each type in detail:

- White-Hat Hackers – A white-hat hacker is a computer expert that focuses on the security aspects of technology. Often, this kind of hacker specializes in testing methods (e.g. penetration testing) to boost and maintain the digital security of a network. If you are a white-hat hacker, you can apply as a security professional to businesses and organizations.

- Black-Hat Hackers – A black-hat hacker, also known as "cracker", accesses machines and networks without permission from the owner. He/she uses his/her skills to attack a target and gain access to it. Often, a cracker attacks computer networks for fun, for profit, for a social cause, or for a political reason. He/she may steal confidential information, delete files, or prevent authorized users from using the system.

CHAPTER 2

THE THINGS YOU NEED TO KNOW ABOUT HACKING

A lot of people want to be a hacker. However, they have no idea what hacking actually means, or where to begin. This chapter will explain the basic concepts related to hacking. Read this material carefully if you want to be a skilled hacker.

- Hacking requires patience – If you want to be a hacker, you need to have a lot of patience. You won't become a hacker overnight. Most hackers spend months studying the tools and techniques they need to attack computer systems. As a beginner, it would be best if you'll start working with a few hacking tools. Work with those tools for several weeks (or even months). By limiting the number of tools you are using, you increase your chances of mastering them.

- Hacking requires knowledge – Hackers know lots of things about computers. They know how to use a computer, how to create a program, how to install applications, and how to get the things they need. Learning all these things would be easy if you have a teacher. However, since most hackers learn by themselves, you need to do some self-studying. Here are things you need to do to gain the prerequisite knowledge:

  o Read – You should read a lot of books related to hacking. These days, textbooks and handbooks that teach hacking skills are available in local and online bookstores.

  o Know how to create programs – Skilled hackers create their own programs. They don't rely on virus repositories to get the hacking tools they need. Actually, if you don't know how to program, other hackers will look down on you. That means you should learn at least one programming language. As a beginner, you should study C or C# first. These languages are easy to understand – you will master them easily.

o Hack – You won't become a hacker if you won't hack computer systems. Reading books and writing your own programs are good, but they can't turn you into the hacker you've been dreaming of. The best (and quickest) way to become a hacker is by practicing your hacking skills on a regular basis.

- Online Searching – Nowadays, almost everything you need to know is available online. Websites (e.g. Wikipedia.com) contain tons of information that can help you in your hacking activities. You don't have to get newspapers, magazines, or encyclopedias anymore. To get any piece of information, you can simply launch a web browser and run an online search.

- Collecting Useful Information – Hackers need to collect information about their target. Specifically, they should get their hands on the target's password and IP address. Let's discuss these in detail:

  o Passwords – This piece of information allows you to access a computer or network. However, the privileges that you can enjoy depend on the user account you are logged in. If you want to gain complete control, you should go for the admin's password.

O IP Addresses – This kind of data can help you identify any machine that is connected to the internet. Basically, websites and network servers transmit data through IP addresses.

CHATER 3

PHISHING TECHNIQUES

The term "phishing" refers to the process of stealing information through deceptive means. When collecting data about their targets, hackers often resort to phishing techniques. This allows them to collect all the information they need while keeping their anonymity.

In this chapter, you'll learn about the best phishing techniques available today. These techniques are:

- Spam Emails – This is one of the most popular techniques among hackers. Here, they send an email to thousands (or even millions) of people and ask them to provide personal information. If any of the victims comply, the hackers will utilize the collected information for illegal actions.

- Instant Messaging – Here, the hacker sends an instant message to his/her potential victims. That message contains a link to a rigged website, which is usually a modified version of a popular site (e.g. Facebook, Twitter, Gmail, etc.). When the victim tries to log in, the site will capture the login information and send it to the hacker.

- Key Loggers – Basically, a "key logger" is a program that records keyboard inputs. This program sends the information to its owner (i.e. the hacker) through the internet. Because of this program, some websites offer virtual keyboards to their customers. This approach allows customers to enter personal data using their mouse.

- Content Injection – In this technique, the hacker alters a certain part of a webpage. Its aim is to encourage the user to go to another website and enter his/her personal information there. "Content Injection" becomes more effective if used on a reliable website.

- Web-based Delivery – This modern technique relies on the principle of MITM (man-in-the-middle). The attacker intercepts the connection between a website and a legitimate user. Then, he/she will capture the data exchanged between the two parties. This technique is extremely effective: it can collect personal and/or confidential data from one or both parties.

CHAPTER 4

HOW TO CRACK PASSWORDS ONLINE

Hackers need to access their target before they launch an attack or penetration test. Without an access to the target, even the brightest hackers cannot do anything. This is the reason why hackers develop a wide range of tools and techniques in gaining access to a targeted machine or network. In this chapter, you'll learn about the most basic way of getting that elusive network access – cracking a user's password.

Once you have cracked a user's password, you'll be able to log in to the network, view/copy/delete important files, install programs, prevent authorized users from logging in, and even shut down the target completely. Thus, you should study this material carefully if you want to be a skilled hacker.

The Two Types of Online Password-Cracking Techniques

Professional hackers divide password cracking-techniques into two types: passive and active. Let's discuss each type in detail:

The Passive Techniques

Hackers use the term "password sniffing" when referring to passive online techniques. These techniques are called "passive" because they prevent the user from detecting the hacker's attempt in cracking the password. You can use them on any type of network (i.e. wired or wireless).

Here are three online passive techniques that you can use:

- Dictionary Attack – With this technique, you will capture the password as it travels through the system and compare it against a word list (also known as "dictionary file"). However, this approach only works on unencrypted passwords. If the password is encrypted (or "hashed"), you need to use special tools to crack the algorithm used in the encryption process.

- MITM (i.e. Man in the Middle) – This technique requires you to install a sniffer between the server and the client. Here, the sniffer will intercept all authentication requests, copy the user's login information, and send the requests to the server.

- Replay Attack – Hackers consider this as one of the simplest password-cracking tricks available today. In a replay attack, the hacker doesn't have to identify the actual password entered by the user. Instead, he/she will just capture the data packets used in the authentication procedure. Then, he/she will just "replay" the authentication process by sending the captured packets.

The Active Techniques

An active password-cracking technique leaves traces of the hacker's attempts. Basically, these techniques entail more risks compared to the passive ones. Here are two active techniques used by modern hackers:

- Password Guessing – This is one of the easiest and simplest techniques that you can use. You'll just guess the user's password using the information you have about that person. The main problem with this technique is that it only works on weak passwords. Also, you have to know some personal information about the user before guessing his/her password.

- Brute-Force Approach – In this technique, you'll enter all possible combinations of letters, numbers, and special characters in order to crack the password. It can crack any password if given sufficient time and processing power. However, this trick is no longer effective. Most servers and websites limit the number of login attempts. Once that limit is reached, the account will be locked to prevent security concerns.

CHAPTER 5

THE BASICS OF PENETRATION TESTING

Penetration testing is the process of studying and attacking a computer network in order to assess its defensive capabilities. Once weaknesses have been found, the attacker should record all of his/her observations and submit some recommendations to the person who hired him/her.

Often, businesses and organizations hire professional hackers to conduct this kind of test. The hacker collects information about the target as if he is a malicious attacker. This way, he can discover all of the attacking avenues that can be used by the bad guys. During a penetration test, the hacker aims to discover the target's vulnerabilities, assess the risks involved, and share his/her recommendations to the business owner or IT manager.

Penetration tests involve several phases. These phases are:

1. Establishing the Rules – During this phase, the hacker needs to determine the following:

   a. The objectives of the test

   b. The things he should and shouldn't attack

   c. The need to let the network admins know about the test

   d. The date/s of the attack/s

   e. Legal Concerns

      i. A hacking procedure can be against the law, even if the target requested for it.

      ii. As an ethical hacker, you should become familiar with the laws (i.e. federal, local, and state) relevant to hacking activities.

   f. The things he/she should submit after completing the test

2. Passive Scanning – Here, the hack needs to collect information about the network owner through outside sources. He/she may use websites, government records, and similar data sources to learn more about his/her

target. The main goal of this phase is to gather sufficient information without establishing any contact between the hacker and the target.

3. Active Scanning – This phase requires the hacker to study the target using his tools. Here are the techniques that you can use during an active scan:

    a. Banner Grabbing

    b. Sniffing of Data Traffic

    c. Social Engineering

    d. Wireless Attacks

4. Attack Surface Analysis – Scan the target to identify its vulnerable ports. Hackers use the following tools and techniques in scanning the target:

    a. Perimeter firewall

    b. Network mapping

    c. Identification of switch and router locations

    d. WAN, LAN, and MAN connections

5. Fingerprinting – In this part of the test, the hacker must identify the following:

a. Open ports

b. User accounts

c. Type of OS (i.e. operating system)

d. Available computer programs

e. Active services

6. Target Selection – The hacker should choose the target/s he/she must attack. The time and resources available to him/her are limited, so it would be impractical (if not impossible) to attack all of the identified weaknesses.

7. Conducting the Attack – Here, the hacker should attack the selected weakness.

8. Enhancing the Privilege – In this phase, the attacker boosts his user privileges. Thus, he will have more control over the targeted network. Professional hackers escalate their user privileges by cracking passwords or launching buffer overflows on a local machine.

9. Recording and Reporting – The hacker needs to record the significant things he discovered. He also needs to record the date of the attack, the tools and techniques he used, as well as the vulnerabilities he exploited. Lastly, he

should submit his own recommendations to help the client in improving its digital defenses.

CHAPTER 6

HOW TO BECOME AN ONLINE SPY

In this chapter, you'll learn how to spy on people online. This material will focus on two channels: Instagram and WhatsApp.

How to Spy Using Instagram

Currently, hackers consider "mSpy" as the best tool for spying on Instagram. This program allows you to track a user's activities in the Instagram network. Basically, mSpy has modern and interesting features that check the action of any Instagram user. With this tool, you can do the things given below:

- See the online content that your target has liked.

- Read your target's comments.

- Determine the location where the photos were uploaded.

- Identify the people that were tagged in the user's uploaded images.

- See detailed information about the content uploaded by your target.

Know Your Target's Perspective

With mSpy, you can view almost anything a person does in the Instagram network. Thus, utilizing this tool can help you identify the point-of-view of your target. You'll know his/her hobbies, preferences, and online antics.

Know What His/Her Friends Think About Him/Her

Just like Facebook, Instagram allows users to like and share the contents uploaded by others. If your target uploads pictures and videos that trigger likes/shares from other people, he is popular.

How to Spy Using WhatsApp

Here are two tricks that you can use to spy on WhatsApp users:

- Track their login schedule – This trick allows you to determine the exact time when a user logs in to his/her WhatsApp account. Let's divide this trick into detailed steps:

  ○ Visit this site to download an app called WhatsDog.

○ Install the app and launch it.

○ The program will ask you to specify a WhatsApp user. Type in the correct information and hit "OK" once you see a pop-up window.

○ The next screen will show you the exact timestamps of your target's login attempts. This program works regardless of the user's account settings.

- Read their messages – This trick allows you to view your target's conversations. It will work even if the person is using AppLock. Here are the things you need to do:

  ○ Get the target's phone and visit this site. Hackers consider this as an excellent tool for spying on WhatsApp users. If you want, you can download the app as an apk file and send it to your target's phone.

  ○ Launch the program and select the right message filtering option. This app allows you to filter messages based on date, chat, or message types.

  ○ Choose the best file type for the output. Most hackers select .txt here.

- The next screen will show you two options for exporting the output. These options are: Email and SD Card. Since you want to keep things simple and discrete, you should choose the "Email" option.

- Access the user's email account, check the Sent folder, and delete the message containing the .txt file. If you don't, your target will know that you have copied his/her messages.

CHAPTER 7

THE MOST DESTRUCTIVE COMPUTER VIRUSES IN HISTORY

In this chapter, you'll learn about the most destructive computer viruses of all time. These malicious programs affected countless computers and resulted to millions of dollars in consumer losses.

1. Melissa – A programmer named David Smith created a malicious program (also known as malware) and called it "Melissa." Melissa was a self-replicating program that used email messages to reach its victims. Once you open an infected email, the virus will install itself onto your machine and send itself to the people listed in your contact list.

2. ILOVEYOU – According to some people, the ILOVEYOU virus came from the Philippines. Similar to the Melissa program, this virus

infected computers through emails. The email that contained this program had an attached text file named "LOVE-LETTER-FOR-YOU". Once it had infected a computer, the ILOVEYOU virus performed the following:

> a. It created multiple copies of itself. Then, it stored the duplicates in the hard drive of the affected machine.
>
> b. It generated files inside the registry key of the machine.
>
> c. It recorded the passwords entered by the user and sent the information to the hacker via email.

3. Klez – This virus raised the standards for newly-created malware. Just like other viruses, it infected computers through email messages. However, Klez was more advanced than Melissa and ILOVEYOU.

The Klez program had three interesting features which made it extremely powerful. These features are:

> a. It can act as a container for other viruses.

b. It can disable the antivirus software of the infected machine and pretend as a malware-protection tool.

c. It can change the "From" field of the email. This process, known as spoofing, makes the target think that the message came from a reliable sender.

4. Code Red – This computer virus infected computers back in 2001. Basically, it took advantage of a weakness found in Windows NT and Windows 2000. The Code Red virus launched a DDoS (i.e. distributed-denial-of-service) attack against the computers within the White House. The attack was successful: it overloaded the infected computers by forcing them to contact the webservers of the White House simultaneously.

5. Nimda – This virus had an unbelievable propagation time. According to authorities, Nimda became the number one malware in just 22 minutes after its release. Nimda considered internet servers as its main targets. Although it was capable of infecting personal computers, its actual objective was to slow down the internet traffic. It propagated itself across countless machines through email messages, similar to other viruses included in this list.

6. Sapphire – In 2003, an internet virus named Sapphire (or Slammer) infected countless machines and caused serious damages. For example, the ATM service of the Bank of America crashed, the 911 service of Seattle went down, and Continental Airlines was forced to cancel flights.

7. MyDoom – The MyDoom virus was a program that can generate "backdoors" in a computer's OS. IT experts say that MyDoom activated twice back in 2004. During the first activation, it launched a DoS (denial-of-service) attack against the infected machines. The second activation, on the other hand, caused the program to stop replicating itself. Even though the replication process had stopped, the backdoors generated during the first part of the attack stayed active.

8. Sasser – This virus attacked computers that run on a Windows OS. Unlike other viruses, Sasser didn't infect its victims through emails. Rather, after installing itself onto a machine, it searched for nearby systems that can be attacked. Sasser contacted nearby networks and forced them to get the virus from an online source.

9. Leap-A – IT experts consider this as the first malware to infect a Mac computer. Leap-A, also called Oompa-A, attacked Macintosh machines

back in 2006. It utilized iChat (i.e. a messaging application) to spread across multiple computers. After infecting one computer, it scanned the contact list of the user and sent corrupted files to all of the addresses found.

10. Storm Worm – People refer to this virus as "Storm Worm" because the subject line of the email that contained it was "230 dead as storm batters Europe". After installing itself onto a computer, it turned the victim into a "bot" (or "zombie"). A zombie machine allows the hacker to do whatever he wants, hence the name.

CHAPTER 8

THE MOST NOTORIOUS COMPUTER
HACKERS IN HISTORY

According to some people, black-hat hackers were born as soon as the first computers were released in the market. Also, some of these techno-buffs have caused more damage than you probably know. Law enforcers haven't caught up with the tools, tricks, and techniques used by these misguided hackers.

In this chapter, you'll discover five of the most notorious hackers to ever live in this planet.

- Vladimir Levin – In 1995, Vladimir Levin hacked the computers of Citibank and stole almost $10,000,000 by transferring the money to different accounts. According to the authorities, Mr. Levin committed the crime without using the internet. Instead of doing an "online" attack, he accessed the communication systems of Citibank and listened to employees and customers discuss bank account details.

- Albert Gonzales – This hacker launched the largest identity theft in history. He stole millions of debit and credit card accounts. According to authorities, Albert Gonzales hacked about 170 million credit and debit cards. Back in 2010, he was found guilty and was sentenced to spend 20 years of his life behind bars.

- Adrian Lamo – Mr. Lamo hacked the IT system of The New York Times back in 2002. The attack allowed him to view confidential information, such as the names of the individuals who had helped in completing the Op-Ed part of the paper.

- Kevin Poulsen – This hacker specialized in hacking telephone networks. The reports say that Mr. Poulsen hacked into a phone network to make sure that he will win a prize from a contest. Also, he allegedly hacked into the phone conversations of a Hollywood actress.

When the FBI started to look for him, Kevin Poulsen hid for about 17 months. Because of his disappearance, the popular TV program named "Unsolved Mysteries" featured him.

That episode triggered a famous hacking event. Just when the TV screens showed a telephone number the viewers could call if they knew anything about Poulsen, the program's telephone lines went dead.

- Gary McKinnon – This Scottish hacker accessed 97 military networks of the US in a span of two years. According to some reports, McKinnon even left an insulting message on the website of the military.

  The most interesting part of McKinnon's hacking quest is his purpose. Instead of stealing money or data, he simply searched for evidences that will prove the existence of aliens. Actually, he claimed that he saw some images of extra-terrestrial spacecrafts in the military's database. However, because his internet connection was too slow, he wasn't able to download any of those images.

CHAPTER 9

HOW TO BECOME A WHITE-HAT HACKER

You probably know that computer hacking can be illegal. This kind of activity often involves unauthorized access to confidential and proprietary information. If you aren't careful, your digital adventures can turn into serious crimes. However, passion is difficult to control. If you really love to hack systems but don't want to break the law, you should become a white-hat hacker.

White-hat hackers serve as security experts and IT consultants for businesses and organizations. They prevent the bad guys from abusing the weak (in some cases). Basically, they ensure that black-hat hackers won't be able to access the computers and networks of companies and organizations.

In this chapter, you'll discover what you need to do in order to become a white-hat hacker.

- Develop soft skills – Hacking involves non-technical stuff. Similar to other IT jobs, being a white-hat hacker needs "soft skills." Here are the things you need to develop:

  ○ Work ethic

  ○ Communication skills

  ○ Problem-solving skills

  ○ Ability to stay dedicated and motivated.

- Make sure that your actions are legal – You are a white-hat hacker. Thus, you should never do any black-hat stuff. Prior to accessing or attacking a network, ensure that you have the owner's permission. Your chances of getting hired as a white-hat hacker will decrease if you'll get incarcerated for black-hat hacking activities.

- Get certified – To become an ethical hacker, you should be a CEH (i.e. Certified Ethical Hacker). This certification involves getting several years of experience working in a security-related IT position and earning the right credentials.

CHAPTER 10

THE SECURITY PROTOCOLS THAT YOU CAN USE EVERYDAY

In this part of the book, you'll discover the security protocols used by computer experts. These protocols, although basic, can help you protect your devices and networks.

1. Make sure that your computer has an antivirus program. Also, update your antivirus program on a regular basis. Hackers release new viruses into the internet each day. Obviously, outdated antivirus software cannot stop these newborn viruses.

2. Create a unique username for each of your devices. When creating a username, don't use any information that is linked to you. For example, if the name of your pet is "Black," and your favorite beverage is coffee, don't use Blackcoffee as your username.

35

3. Create a unique password for your devices. Obviously, you should never create passwords that are connected to you personally. Don't use your pet's or wife's name as your password, regardless of your love for them. The last thing you want to do is allow a black-hat hacker to use your beloved's name in wrecking your machine/network.

4. Memorize your login credentials and don't write them anywhere. With this approach, hackers won't be able to get your username and/or password even if they turn your room or office upside down. If you have "memory problems," however, and you really need to write your login information for future reference, make sure that that slip of paper is stored somewhere safe. Don't leave that note on your table.

5. Don't play around with the security settings of your devices. If you don't know what you're doing, don't change the security settings of your machines. Those settings, which are often set in "Recommended" mode, are there to protect your computers and mobile gadgets from hackers and malicious programs.

6. Change the login credentials of your router. All routers have a default login/password. Since these pieces of information can easily be

cracked, you should change it as soon as you can. Follow the tips given above in creating a username and password for your router.

CHAPTER 11

THE BEST TOOLS AND WEBSITES FOR HACKERS

In this chapter, you'll discover the best tools and sites that modern hackers use. By reading this material, you'll familiarize yourself with the best tools and resources available to you.

This chapter consists of two parts, namely: tools and websites.

The Tools

- IPSCAN – This tool, also known as Angry IP Scanner, can help you identify your target's ports and IP addresses. Ports serve as doorways for hackers – you can use them to access the targeted machine or network. IP addresses, on the other hand, act as identification numbers. These addresses can help you identify the machines connected to a network.

- Burp Suite – This suite of applications plays an important role in any hacker's toolkit. It contains many tools that can make your hacking activities easy and simple. For instance, its "spider" component can identify the vulnerable pages and parameters of a site. Thus, you should use this tool if you're planning to launch a hacking attack against a website.

- Metasploit – This powerful tool can detect the weaknesses of any target. Because of its effectiveness, hackers (i.e. both white-hat and black-hat) include Metasploit in their toolkit. This software also has excellent evasion features – it can help you cover the tracks of your "dirty" work.

- Ettercap – This tool is extremely popular among hackers. Its main purpose is to help hackers in facilitating MITM (man-in-the-middle) attacks.

- Kali Linux – This application comes with interface and distribution tools. It has excellent hardware and is compatible with different computer environments. Basically, Kali Linux is an operating system that you can launch from a thumb drive or a CD. It has a built-in toolkit that can crack passwords, establish bogus networks, and identify network weaknesses.

The Websites

- www.hacking-tutorial.com – This website proves that "perfect English" plays a minor role in learning. The writers share excellent tips, tricks, and lessons to countless people worldwide. Even though their writing skills are not "award-winning", they can provide you with topnotch instructions that you won't find elsewhere. If you're looking for relevant, informative, and easy-to-read hacking lessons, this is the perfect site for you.

- www.evilzone.org – The name of this website is quite intimidating. However, it's not a cult or anything like that. It's actually a large online community of hackers. Currently, it has about 20,000 registered members and about 70,000 posts. If you have any question regarding hacking or programming, this site can provide the answer you're looking for.

- www.hackaday.com – This blog offers articles, instructional videos, and a large online community. Aside from online hacking techniques, this blog can teach you how to hack physical devices such as game consoles and digital cameras.

CHAPTER 12

THE BENEFITS OF BEING A WHITE-HAT HACKER

In this chapter, you'll discover the benefits offered by the CEH certification. As you probably know, this certification is an absolute requirement for everyone who wants to be a professional white-hat hacker. CEH stands for Certified Ethical Hacker.

By taking the CEH course, you will:

- Know how to think like a black-hat hacker – Once you've completed the CEH course, you'll know how malicious hackers launch their attacks. You want to stop the bad guys so you need to know how they do their stuff. With this information, you can easily detect, stop, and prevent hacking attacks.

- Learn how malicious programs work and evolve – You will also know how malware works. As a white-hat hacker, you should be familiar with viruses, worms, and Trojans. Stopping a virus is impossible if you don't know how that virus works. Keep in mind that you can't rely on Avira or McAfee once you've become a pro. Those programs can help, but you have to arm yourself with the actual knowledge on how to stop malicious programs from infesting and destroying networks.

- Discover the tools and techniques used by the pros – By being certified as an ethical (or white-hat) hacker, you'll familiarize yourself with the techniques and programs used by professional hackers. Since you are dealing with computers and programs, abstract knowledge isn't enough. You need to use certain tools to do what you need to do. For instance, knowledge about ports won't help you detect the open ports of a system. You still need to run port scanners to achieve your goal.

CHAPTER 13

HOW TO HACK OR PROTECT A WIRELESS NETWORK

This chapter will focus on wireless networks. In particular, it will explain how you can launch and prevent wireless hacking attacks.

Hacking a Wireless Network

All wireless networks have two inherent weaknesses: weak encryption and weak configuration. Weak encryption results from the issues with WEP and WPA security. Weak configuration, on the other hand, results from poor practices regarding network administration. It usually involves default system settings, absence of security protocol, and usage of weak passwords.

These days, when hacking tools are available all over the internet, attacking wireless networks has become extremely easy. Here are two tools that you can use to hack wireless networks:

- Aircrack – With this program, you can crack WPA and WPE passwords. It uses the latest algorithms to crack the captured data packets. You can download it from the following site: www.aircrack-ng.org.

- Airsnort – This tool can crack WEP passwords by capturing and analyzing data packets sent in a network. It works for Windows and Linux computers. You can download it without spending any money. Just visit this site and click on the download link.

Protecting a Wireless Network

- Change the password of your router – Every router comes with a default password. Hackers know this simple fact: they are always on the lookout for vulnerable wireless connections in their surroundings. Thus, if you want to protect your network, the first thing you should do is change the router's password.

- Change and hide the name of your network – Hackers have access to a lot of password-cracking tools. Thus, changing the password of your router isn't enough. You also need to change your network's name and hide it from other people. Routers come with a predetermined name – hackers will have an easy time accessing your network if you will use the default router name. After changing the name, hide it from other wireless devices. The steps for changing and hiding the network name varies from router to router: you need to read the manual that came with your device.

- Use MAC addresses to protect your devices – This is probably one of the best ways to prevent hacking attacks. Here, you'll set your network so that it accepts certain devices only: gadgets that aren't listed won't be able to connect to the network. Here are the things you need to do:

  1. Launch your computer's command prompt and enter ipconfig/all.

  2. The screen will show you a lot of information. Search for the line that says "Physical Address". That is the MAC address of that machine.

  3. Do the same thing on other computers.

  4. Once you have collected the MAC addresses of your devices, log in to your

router and set the filtering for MAC addresses. The steps involved in that process vary from router to router. Check the manual that came with your router to determine the exact procedure.

CONCLUSION

Thank you for reading this Book.

I hope this book was able to teach you the basics of hacking. The topics included in this material were carefully chosen to help you become a skilled hacker. The tools, tricks and techniques you've read about in this book are guaranteed to assist you in achieving your dreams of becoming a security expert. Most of the programs and websites discussed here are available for free. That means you can establish your hacking toolkit and library without shelling out any money.

This book discussed the differences between black-hat and white-hat hackers. By citing these differences, this book tries to help you in making the choice between these two types of hackers.

Additionally, this material explained the basics of penetration testing. "Penetration testing," the most popular method of checking a network's defenses, plays an important role in the field of digital security. If you want to become a professional white-hat hacker, you should study that topic carefully. This book contains explanations and detailed instructions on how to conduct a penetration test on a network.

Thank you and good luck!

Steven Dunlop

THE END.....

ABOUT THE AUTHOR

Steven Dunlop is an entrepreneur who sees a bright future. He is a professional author dedicated to studying and executing in peak performance strategies, with a specialty in business, health and the world's best success strategies. He also pursues a extensive range of extracurricular activities that lead him to experience life changing adventures and new discoveries.

Steven has become a master at focusing his energy to deliver world class content that is helpful, easy to understand and enjoyable to read. He was born in 1989 and graduated from Bristol University with degrees in Business   and   English.

Steven has been studying and implementing self development strategies for the last 8 years, spending thousands of dollars and tremendous amounts of time and energy in this endeavor. His two favorite role models are Tony   Robbins   and   Arnold   Schwarzenegger.

"It is in your moments of decision that your destiny is shaped."–Tony-Robbins

"Strength does not come from winning. Your struggles develop your strengths. When you go through hardships and decide not to surrender, that is strength."-Arnold Schwarzenegger

"The path to success is to take massive, determined action."-Tony-Robbins

Steven is a reader first and foremost, he is also a fitness enthusiast, long time amateur body builder, and a passionate writer. He enjoys writing on subjects that will truly be helpful to thousands of people. Steven has been very successful throughout his life in competitive situations, such as in sales, track and field, rugby, strength training, running businesses, brewing beer, and anything else that he is currently focusing his attention on. Steven has led many teams to victory over the years and during that time has acquired a powerful set of motivational and leadership skills. Steven attributes his success to his ability to focus his time, energy and strategic thinking skills to a particular goal in a relentless manner until it has been accomplished.

Steven makes a strong effort every day to expand his knowledge so that he can bring you world class content each and every time. You can contact Steven at kindleshack@gmail.com

Thanks for reading!